Best of IN RECITAL® **SOLOS**

ABOUT THE SERIES • A NOTE TO THE TEACHER

Best of In Recital® Solos is a series that focuses on fabulous solo repertoire, intended to motivate your students. The fine composers of this series have created musically engaging pieces, and the wide range of styles in this six-book series is sure to please any student! It will help you to plan students' recital repertoire easily. This series can also be used as weekly motivation and fun, as well as for sight-reading! You will find original solos that emphasize different musical and technical issues, giving you the selections to accommodate all of your student's needs. These fabulous solos are from the following series: *In Recital® Throughout the Year, Volumes 1 and 2; In Recital® with Jazz, Blues, and Rags; In Recital® with Timeless Hymns; In Recital® with Classical Themes; In Recital® with All Time Favorites;* and *In Recital® with Popular Music.*

Go to inside-back cover for information on downloading free recordings for this book.

Production: Frank J. Hackinson
Production Coordinators: Peggy Gallagher and Philip Groeber
Cover Design: Terpstra Design, San Francisco, CA
Cover Illustrations: Keith Criss, Marcia Donley, and Sophie Library
Engraving: Tempo Music Press, Inc.
Printer: Tempo Music Press, Inc.

ISBN-13: 978-1-61928-098-4

ORGANIZATION OF THE SERIES
BEST OF IN RECITAL® SOLOS

The series is carefully leveled into the following six categories: Early Elementary, Elementary, Late Elementary, Early Intermediate, Intermediate, and Late Intermediate. Each of the works has been selected for its artistic as well as its pedagogical merit.

Book Two — Elementary, reinforces the following concepts:

- In addition to basic notes, such as quarter, half, dotted half, and whole notes, their corresponding rests are also used.

- Students play tied notes, *legato* and *staccato* articulations, accents, up-beats, first and second endings, a few chords, and blocked intervals.

- Students play pieces in five-finger hand positions as well as pieces outside the usual five-finger positions.

- Most of the pieces call for limited use of hands-together playing.

- Basic musical terminology and symbols: *crescendo*, *decrescendo*, *ritardando*, *fermata*, *mezzo piano*, *mezzo forte*, *pianissimo*, *fortissimo*, *accent*, 8va, pedal, *poco rit.*, *D.C. al Fine*, and *loco*.

- Students play in a variety of different keys (written using accidentals instead of key signatures).

TABLE OF CONTENTS

Mist in the Moonlight

Elizabeth W. Greenleaf

FJH2243

Scarecrow Scherzando

Mary Leaf

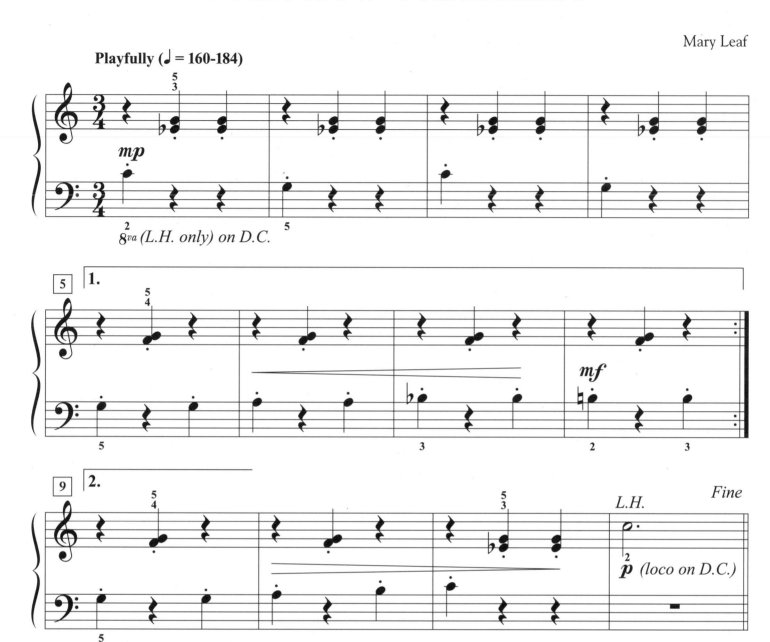

Teacher Duet: (*Student plays one octave higher*)

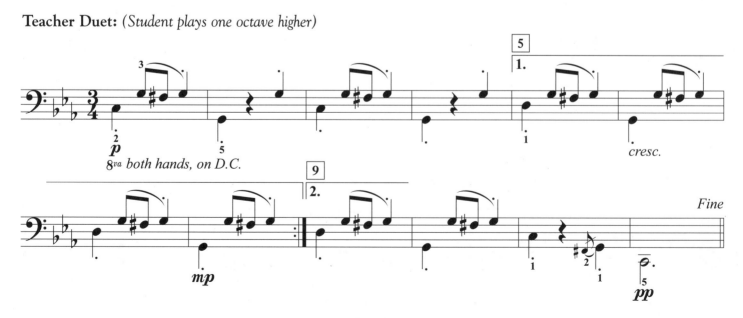

FJH2243

for Ross Neumann

Highland Jig

Mary Leaf

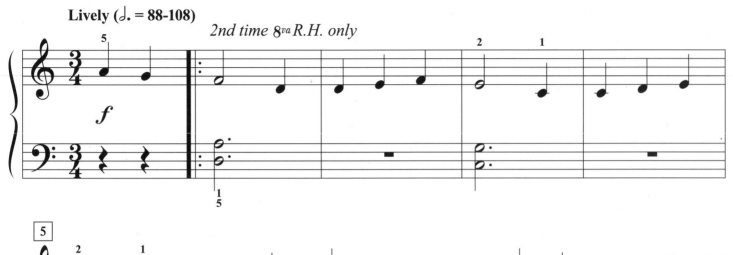

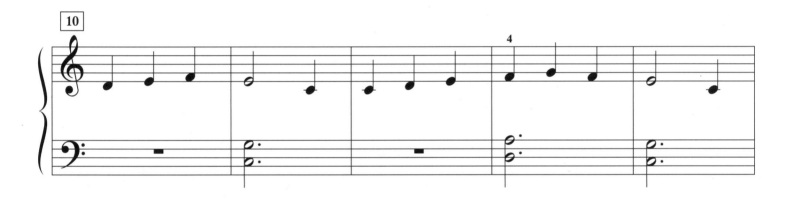

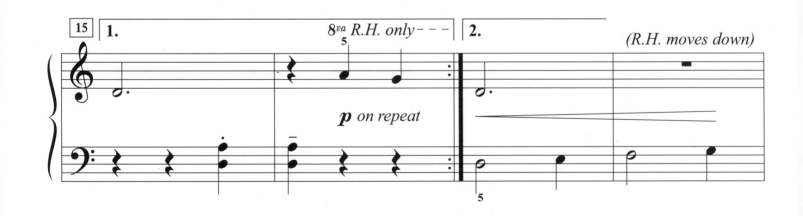

FJH2243

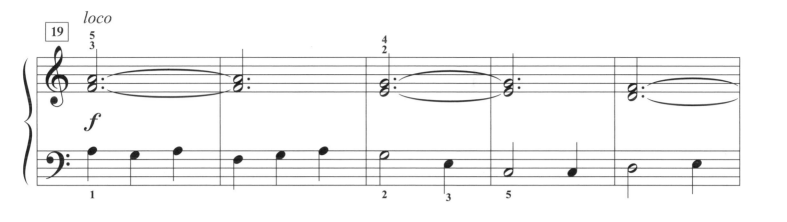

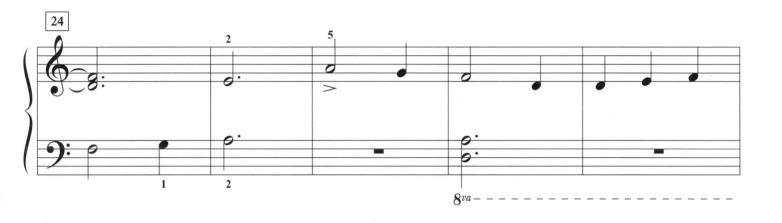

Traffic Jam

Kevin Olson

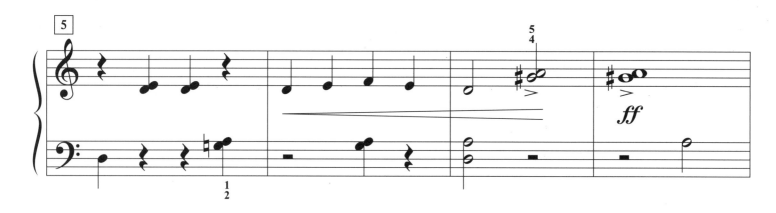

FJH2243

D.C. al Fine

Halloween Sounds

Elizabeth W. Greenleaf

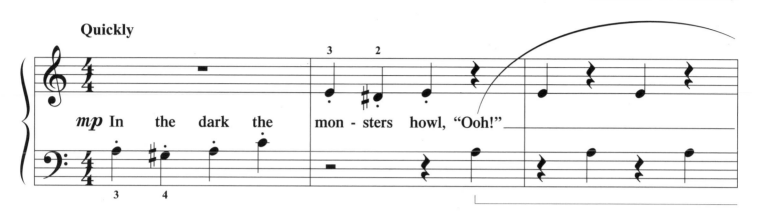

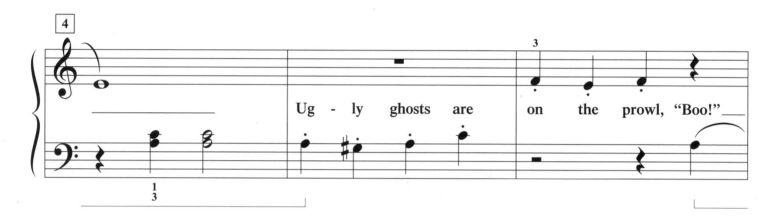

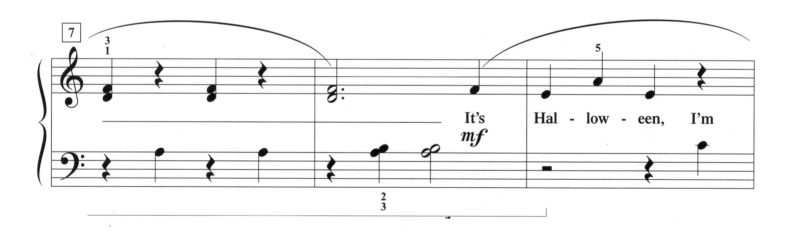

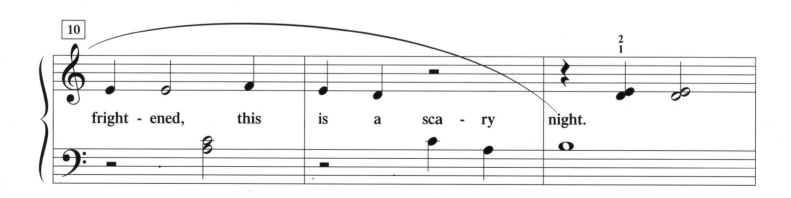

FJH2243

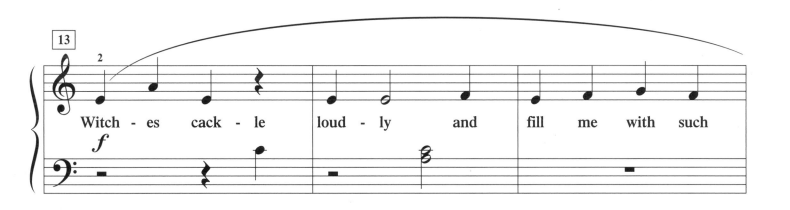

Witch - es cack - le loud - ly and fill me with such

fright! Ev - 'ry - where I look a - bout I

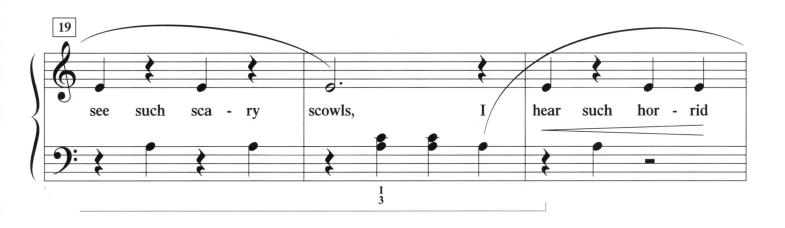

see such sca - ry scowls, I hear such hor - rid

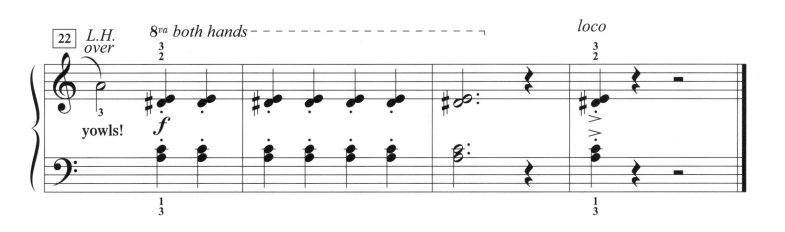

yowls!

Rockin' the Blues

Edwin McLean

With a powerful Rock beat (no swing) ($\bigcirc$ = ca. 104)

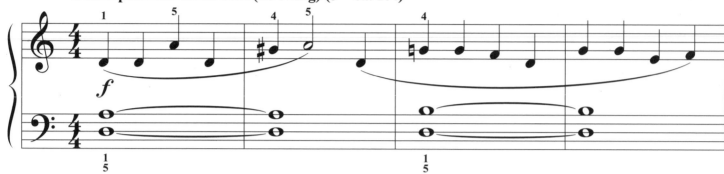

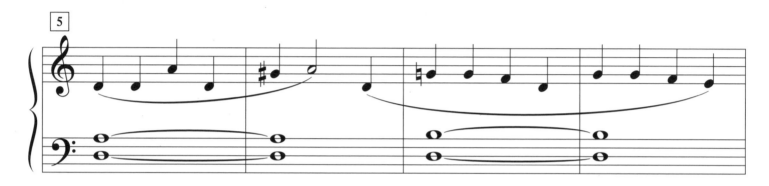

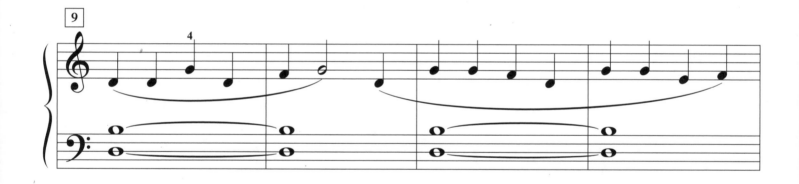

Teacher Duet: *(Student plays one octave higher)*

FJH2243

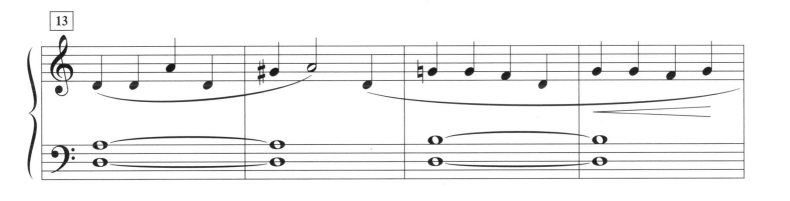

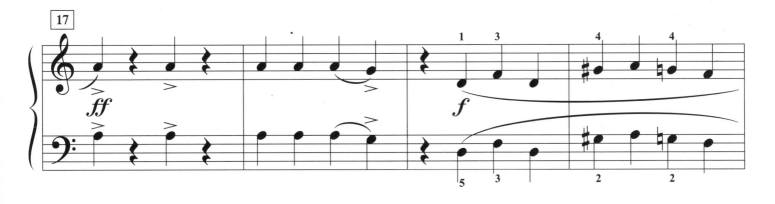

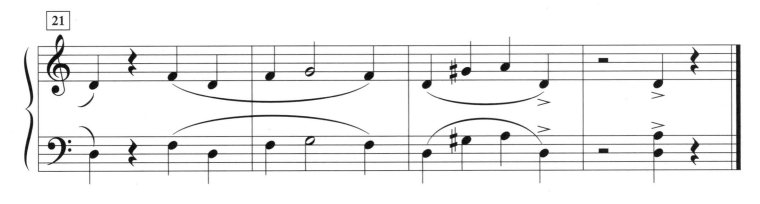

Symphony No. 5

(Opus 67, Movement One)

Ludwig van Beethoven
arr. Robert Schultz

FJH2243

The Japanese Koto*

Christopher Goldston

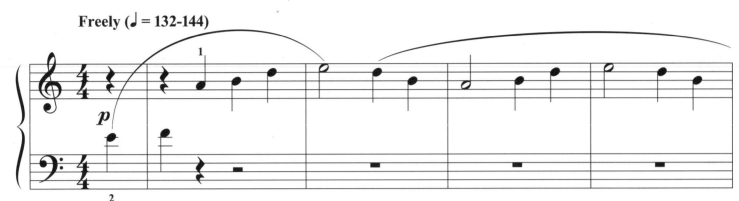

press down the right (damper) pedal throughout

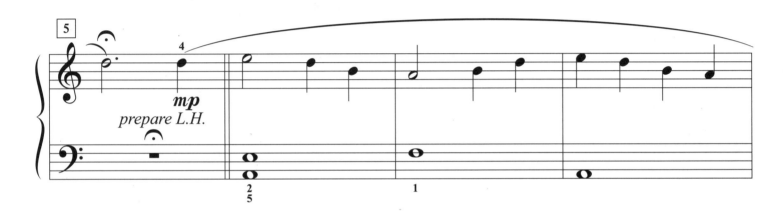

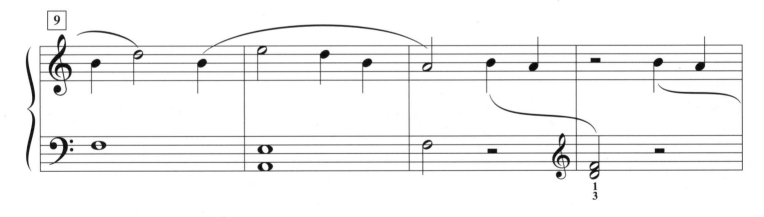

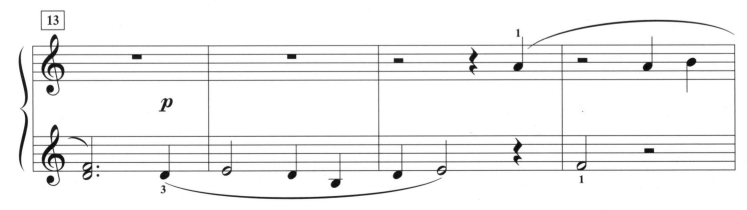

* *The Koto is a harp with 13 strings.*

FJH2243

* Optional: 15ma lower

Ragtag Rag

Robert Schultz

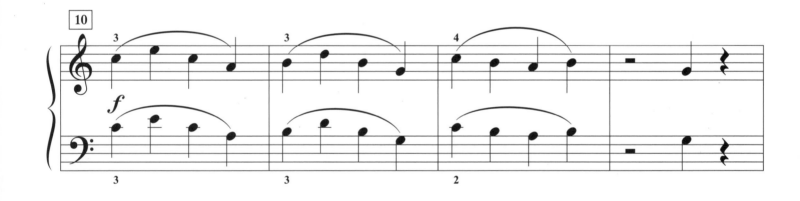

Teacher Duet: (*Student plays one octave higher*)

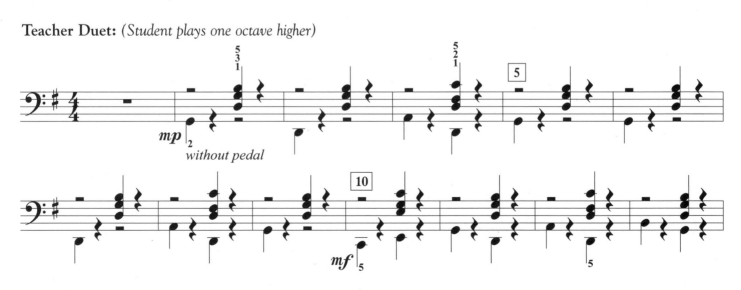

FJH223

Electric Blues

Kevin Olson

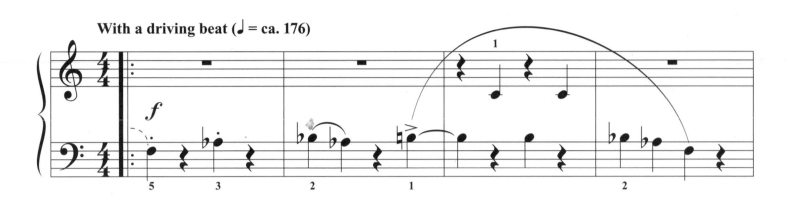

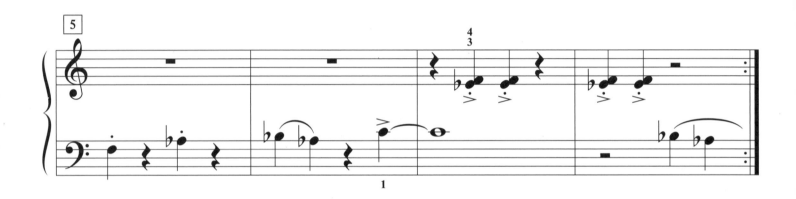

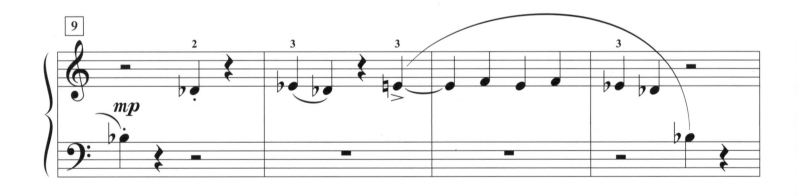

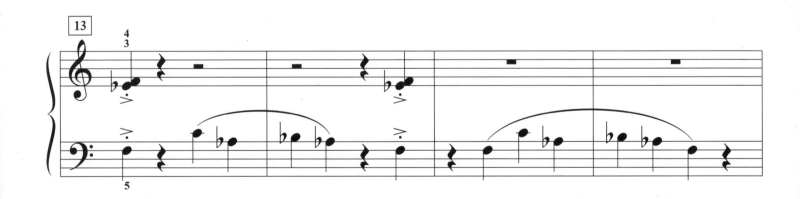

FJH2243

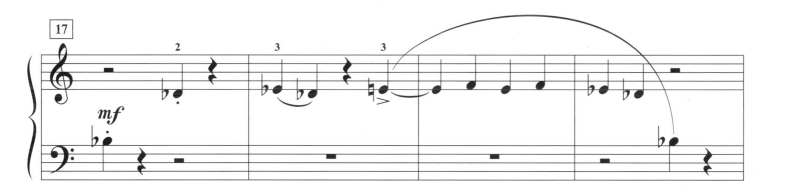

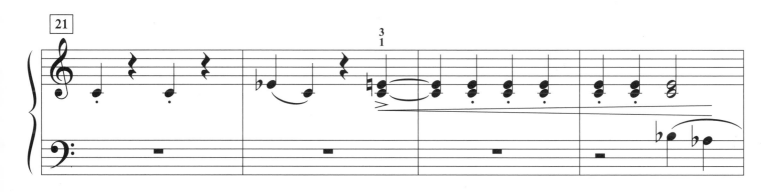

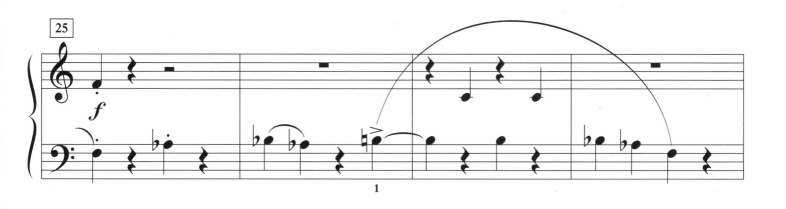

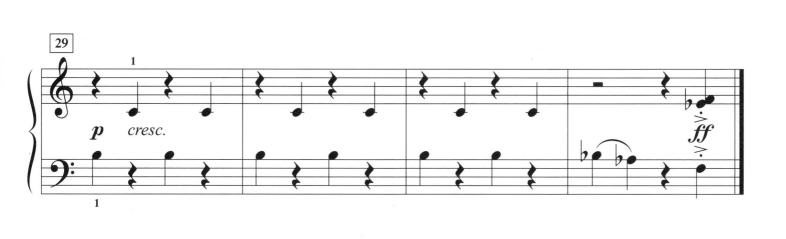

Un viento caliente

(A Warm Wind)

Edwin McLean

Teacher Duet: (*Student plays one octave higher*)

FJH2243

Danny Boy

Frederick Edward Weatherly
arr. Edwin McLean

With a light bounce (♩ = ca. 126-138)

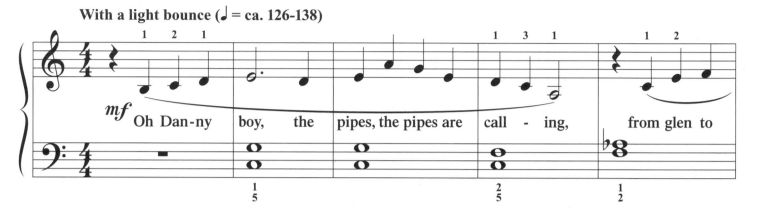

Oh Dan-ny boy, the pipes, the pipes are call - ing, from glen to

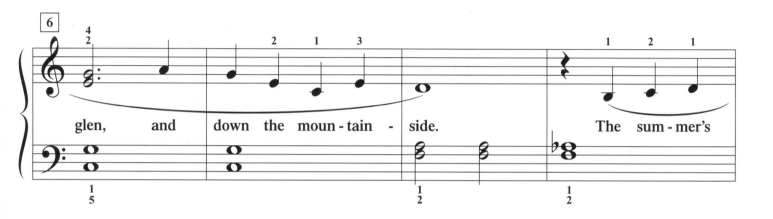

glen, and down the moun-tain - side. The sum-mer's

Teacher Duet: (*Student plays one octave higher*)

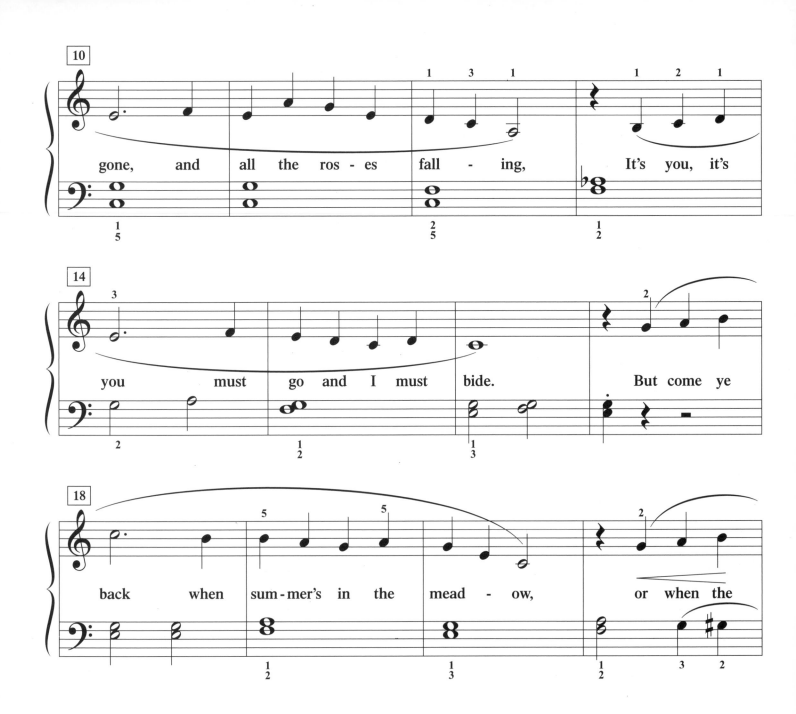

gone,   and   all the ros - es fall - ing,   It's you, it's

you   must   go and I must   bide.   But come ye

back   when   sum - mer's in the   mead - ow,   or when the

FJH2243

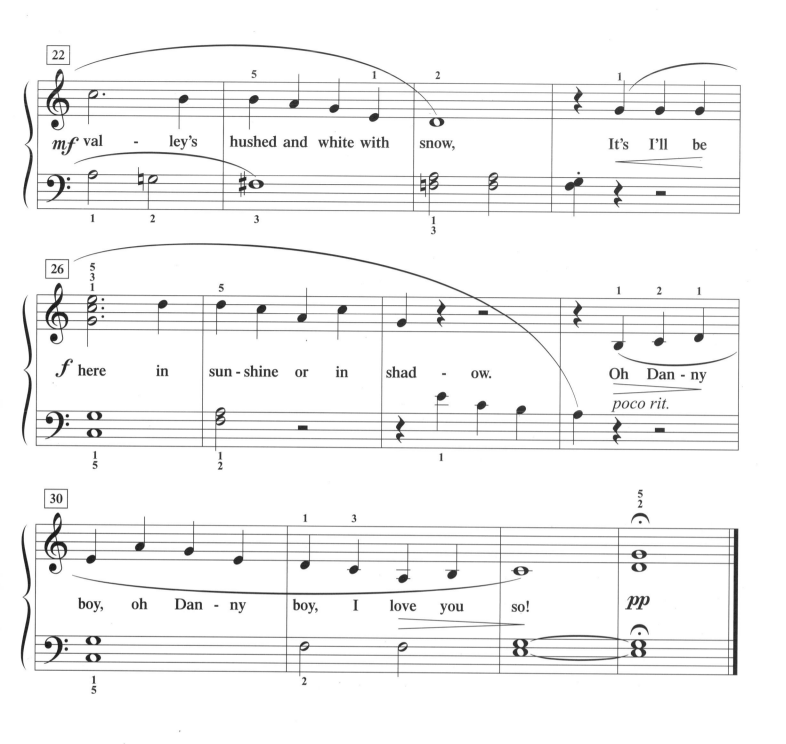

ABOUT THE COMPOSERS AND ARRANGERS

Christopher Goldston

Christopher Goldston holds a Master of Music degree in piano performance and pedagogy from Northwestern University, and a Bachelor of Music degree in piano performance from the University of North Carolina–Greensboro. He lives in Chicago, Illinois, and has taught at Sherwood Conservatory of Music and Harper College. In 1991, Mr. Goldston received the National Federation of Music Clubs Lynn Freeman Olson Composition Award for his first composition, *Night Train*. Since then, he has written numerous pieces for piano, voice, and chamber ensemble, including *Thesis for Wind Quintet*, which won the 1993 North Carolina State Music Teachers Association Collegiate Composition Contest. Mr. Goldston has taught piano for over ten years and enjoys composing and arranging pieces for his students. Many of them have created pieces of their own under his guidance and have received top prizes in state competitions. Mr. Goldston has also served as chair of the composition contest for Illinois State Music Teachers Association and MTNA East Central Division.

Elizabeth W. Greenleaf

Elizabeth W. Greenleaf received a Piano Teaching Certificate and a Bachelor of Music degree in composition from Florida State University, and a Master of Music degree in piano performance from Louisiana State University. Elizabeth has been active as a composer, performer, and teacher for over twenty-five years. She has performed many recitals, both as an accompanist for instrumentalists and singers, and as a chamber music player. Her students have ranged from preschoolers to senior citizens, and she has taught at all levels from beginning to advanced. Recently retired from teaching, Elizabeth enjoys composing to meet the needs of students. Her music has received high praise from top teachers throughout the country.

Mary Leaf

Mary Leaf is an independent piano teacher specializing in early elementary through intermediate level students. She enjoys writing music that is descriptive, expressive, imaginative, and fun, while still being musically sound. Mary received a music education degree from the University of Washington and has done continuing education in pedagogy at North Dakota State University. She is active in her local Music Teachers Association, is a member of NDMTA, MTNA, the National Federation of Musicians, and the National Guild of Piano Teachers. She has also been active in the area as a collaborative pianist and accompanist. Mary and her husband Ron have five grown children and four grandchildren, and reside in Bismarck, North Dakota. They enjoy reading, jigsaw puzzles, sudoku, traveling, and hiking together.

Edwin McLean

Edwin McLean is a composer living in Chapel Hill, North Carolina. He is a graduate of the Yale School of Music, where he studied with Krzysztof Penderecki and Jacob Druckman. He also holds a master's degree in music theory and a bachelor's degree in piano performance from the University of Colorado. Mr. McLean has authored over 200 publications for The FJH Music Company, ranging from *The FJH Classic Music Dictionary* to original works for pianists from beginner to advanced. His highly-acclaimed works for harpsichord have been performed internationally and are available on the Miami Bach Society recording, *Edwin McLean: Sonatas for 1, 2, and 3 Harpsichords*. His 2011 solo jazz piano album *Don't Say Goodbye* (CD1043) includes many of his advanced works for piano published by FJH. Edwin McLean began his career as a professional arranger. Currently, he is senior editor for The FJH Music Company Inc.

ABOUT THE PIECES AND COMPOSERS

Kevin Olson

Kevin Olson is an active pianist, composer, and member of the piano faculty at Utah State University, where he teaches piano literature, pedagogy, and accompanying courses. In addition to his collegiate teaching responsibilities, Kevin directs the Utah State Youth Conservatory, which provides weekly group and private piano instruction to more than 200 pre-college community students. The National Association of Schools of Music has recently recognized the Conservatory as a model for pre-college piano instruction programs. Before teaching at Utah State, he was on the faculty at Elmhurst College near Chicago and Humboldt State University in northern California.

A native of Utah, Kevin began composing at age five. When he was twelve, his composition, *An American Trainride,* received the Overall First Prize at the 1983 National PTA Convention at Albuquerque, New Mexico. Since then he has been a Composer in Residence at the National Conference on Keyboard Pedagogy, and has written music commissioned and performed by groups such as the American Piano Quartet, Chicago a cappella, the Rich Matteson Jazz Festival, MTNA (Music Teachers National Association), and several piano teacher associations around the country. Kevin maintains a large piano studio, teaching students of a variety of ages and abilities. Many of the needs of his own piano students have inspired more than 100 books and solos published by The FJH Music Company Inc., which he joined as a writer in 1994.

Robert Schultz

Robert Schultz, composer, arranger, and editor, has achieved international fame during his career in the music publishing industry. The Schultz Piano Library, established in 1980, has included more than 500 publications of classical works, popular arrangements, and Schultz's original compositions in editions for pianists of every level from the beginner through the concert artist. In addition to his extensive library of published piano works, Schultz's output includes original orchestral works, chamber music, works for solo instruments, and vocal music.

Schultz has presented his published editions at workshops, clinics, and convention showcases throughout the United States and Canada. He is a long-standing member of ASCAP and has served as president of the Miami Music Teachers Association. Mr. Schultz's original piano compositions and transcriptions are featured on the compact disc recordings *Visions of Dunbar* and *Tina Faigen Plays Piano Transcriptions,* released on the ACA Digital label and available worldwide. His published original works for concert artists are noted in Maurice Hinson's *Guide to the Pianist's Repertoire, Third Edition.* He currently devotes his full time to composing and arranging. In-depth information about Robert Schultz and The Schultz Piano Library is available at the Website www.schultzmusic.com.